How the Violin Plays the Violinist

How the Violin Plays the Violinist

A Guide for Violin Students, Teachers, and Parents of Violinists

Written and Illustrated by
Cate Howard

InkWell Publishing
Arlington, MA

Copyright 2008 by Cate Howard

All rights reserved. This book or parts thereof, may not be reproduced or transmitted in any form or by any means electronic or mechanical including recording, photocopying or any information storage and retrieval system without the written permission of the author.

Published by

InkWell Publishing
Arlington, MA

ISBN: 978-0-9768812-4-7

Printed in the United States of America

Pencil sketches by Cate Howard

To Mom and Dad
with love and gratitude

for nurturing my sensitivity, curiosity
and spirit of adventure,

for teaching me to love and respect
fellow human beings,

for opening my eyes to appreciate
the beauty of our planet,

and for giving me my first violin!

Contents

Acknowledgements ix
Preface xi
Introduction xvii

1 How the Violin Plays the Body

Introduction 3
Know Your Body 5
What the Violin Asks of the Player's Body 11
Discovering and Maintaining Balance in the Violinist's Body 17
Physical Injury and the Practice of Yoga 30

2 How the Violin Plays the Mind

Introduction 37
Awareness 39
Objectivity 41
Acceptance and Allowance 43
    Mis-takes 45
Intention 49

3 Integrating the Violin with Our Entire Being

Introduction 55
Tapping into the Resources Within 57
    Home Is Where the Heart Is 57
    Breathing 61
Playing from Our Inner Song 65

Conclusion 69

Sources 71

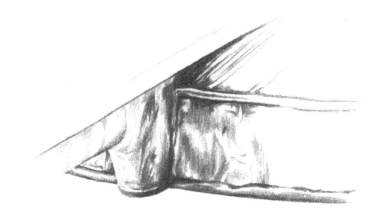

Acknowledgments

The greatest constancy, love and encouragement in all I do has undoubtedly come from my family – Lelia, Wendy, Jeremy, Tim, Mom and Dad.

Friends and colleagues: There are far too many of you to gratefully acknowledge each and every one individually. For sharing your knowledge and experience, and for nurturing me through the completion of this work, heartfelt thanks to Dr. Karen Way, Elizabeth Bunker, Carolyn Megan, and the Fritz family. My photo models Landon, Maddy, and Ryan. My manuscript readers – thank you for your willingness to share your impressions and suggestions with honesty and objectivity, sprinkled with encouragement: Carol Gupta, Enid Wood, Linda Case, Marylou Speaker Churchill, Kato Havas, Ronda Cole, Ed Kreitman, Magdalena Richter, Dr. Reuben Bell.

Special thanks to Jeremy Howard and Julia Meyerson for graphic suggestions and adjustments. To my editor Pauline Kelly – I am very grateful for the clarity (detail and big picture) which have emerged from our work together, and for your commitment to preserving my voice throughout this process.

Always close to my heart, I would also like to acknowledge posthumously, Sarah Megan for her great love as a friend, musician, and the inspiration she left with me: for anything we may feel motivated to do in our lives, now is the time!

To my past and present students and their parents: you have provided a wealth of experiences for me, and I have grown along with you through our many adventures with the violin. I thank you for your commitment, and for entrusting me with your training as young musicians.

My teachers, professors and violin mentors – those who inspired the development of my own skill, proficiency and art – now forever part of my playing and teaching: Yvonne Tait, Doris Strother, Harry Cawood, Alan Solomon, Jascha Brodsky, Christiane Hutcap, Igor Ozim, Linda Fiore, Ronda Cole, and Linda Case.

Preface

For centuries, the beauty and magic of the violin has captivated makers of the instrument, players of the instrument, and listeners. The violin has the power to inspire fascination and curiosity, while demanding integrity and excellence from its players. The expressive tone produced by a violin and its player is capable of touching the very core of one's being, drawing in the violinist and listeners alike.

As players, most of us initially approach the violin as an inanimate object which we bring to life by performing certain actions, for example, by running our fingers over its fingerboard or by pulling the bow across its strings. It is as if we train the instrument to do what we want. It is as if we make it play: **The violinist plays the violin**.

True, yet, when I reflect on my life as a violinist, I realize that whenever I am working with the instrument, the violin and I actually share interactive roles – myself to the instrument and the instrument to me. For any energy I put into initiating vibration through the instrument, there is a return of energy to me as the player and, more expansively, to the listening world beyond.

The violin plays the violinist in the sense that through playing this instrument one awakens and activates connections in one's entire self – body, mind, and spirit. The violin is instrumental both as a tool and as a means of teaching us to better know, understand, and express ourselves.

Years of playing, studying, and teaching this instrument have generated an abundance of experiences in my life. I have had the privilege of gathering a wealth of insights from many fine teachers and mentors who nurtured me professionally. My connection with the violin has in turn served to connect me with countless, wonderful human beings. My journey has taken me on adventures to many parts of the planet. Even as a young child, the tone of the violin and playing this instrument provided me with glimpses of, and have taken me closer to, that which exists beyond time and space. Playing and teaching is very close to my heart. With the violin and bow in my hands I am able to express my innermost being with freedom and honesty.

About eight years ago, I received my first letter from a parent suggesting I write a book. In subsequent years, similar requests followed from a growing number of students, parents of students, friends, and colleagues. These encouragements, along with my own love of learning, playing and teaching the violin have inspired and stimulated the writing of this book.

It is my hope that sharing the concepts presented through text and illustrations in *How the Violin Plays the Violinist*, might translate into a more competent, satisfying delivery of music for you, the violinist, your students, or (in the case of parents) for your young musicians.

This guide is not intended as a methodology, nor is it designed to give specific technical information to violinists. Its purpose, rather, is to:

- ❖ throw light on the nature of the physiological demands the violin places on our bodies

- ❖ offer physical exercises to balance and/or rebalance our systems

- ❖ supply ideas for using our bodies and minds in holistic ways to prevent injury, or to recover from violin-related injuries

- ❖ be an informational source for healthful attitudes toward our playing

- ❖ suggest methods of integrating our entire being (body-mind-spirit) as practicing and performing musicians

Playing the violin informs the
artist-musician's whole being.

Introduction

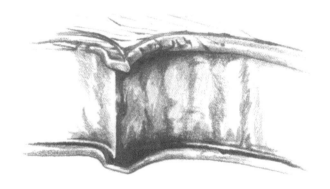

The violin is instrumental both as a tool and as a means of teaching us to better know, understand, and express ourselves.

Playing, studying, practicing, and performing as a musician awakens and activates connections in one's entire self – body, mind, and spirit.

We live much of our early childhood years in the sensory realm. Our **brain** receives and pieces together input from the environment, and our **body** learns to respond and perform actions based on this input. Over time, these learned actions become increasingly refined in control and coordination, allowing us to perform amazingly intricate tasks.

Our **minds** sift through thoughts and emotions, concepts and feelings. Here we have free will, choice in response and reactions, rationality, and the power of directing energy through intention. The mind is also where perception is active – perception of self (including our physical existence and beyond) and the interpretation of life around us.

Our **spirit** is our essence, or the heart of our being. On this level of existence we are able to receive AND generate the energy necessary to express what is creative or inspirational.

> A musician is one who loves the play
> and creation of sound.

Sound is the energetic vibration of molecules transmitted in the form of waves.

Through actions in our body, a musician is able to generate energy through their instrument. Vibrations in the form of sound waves are thereby emitted. Once these waves reach our ears, they are transmitted further in the form of pressure waves, which effect physical changes in the ear's components before being converted into nerve impulses. The energy from these impulses registers as "sound" in the brain. Both the right hemisphere (sensory area) and the left hemisphere (motor area) of the cerebrum's temporal lobe play a role in distinguishing the qualities or attributes of sound. The effect of sound evokes an emotional response and gives rise to thoughts in the mind.

Beyond the body and mind, sound touches the spirit. In this center of our being, one may feel moved and inspired to create and re-create – to invite more play. Spiritual inspiration and our love of playing give rise to a new energy, which then cycles back through the mind to the body. This energy motivates the continuation of sound production through the vehicle of our instrument.

For musicians, the connection of body, mind and spirit with the instrument exposes us to conditions stimulating growth in our **whole person**. Curiosity about how the instrument works or how it makes certain sounds leads us to make discoveries about ourselves. We grow in confidence as our ability develops. We receive encouragement from our families and teachers. We establish habits of daily practice where we begin to understand commitment and responsibility. We begin to focus energy and attention. Through performance, we learn to share our musical discoveries with a listening audience.

Any undertaking that taps into this many facets of our being will undoubtedly also carry with it **challenges** and **life lessons**. There will be times when we long for freedom from the apparent limitations of our body, or perhaps times when we are frustrated with the complexity of the instrument. We may even find ourselves annoyed with the composer who appears to be making our lives so difficult! And we all know what it feels like to experience phases when we'd almost rather help wash the dishes than get on with practicing!

When we feel negative, stuck, disillusioned, so frustrated we want to throw the violin out the window(!), or, perhaps we sustain an injury related to playing the violin – stay with it. Do not give up! These moments can in fact provide the richest opportunities for profound personal realizations and growth. By recognizing and accepting that we will be asked time and again in our lives to step out of our comfort zone, and by knowing we have choices in how we view these feelings or occurrences, we can turn any experience around.

> A violin can be a truly masterful teacher!

In your journey through this book, consider what mind and body habits you practice, what patterns you give energy to, and what neurological connections you reinforce. What are the changes you long for? Do you wish for more clarity, courage, calmness, freedom? Do you wish for more physical ease? Consider embracing the premise that **anything is possible.** Dare to dream big!

The first part of this book is *How the Violin Plays the Body*. In this section, you will find an introduction to anatomy, general ideas on understanding the physical demands the instrument places on a violinist's body, developing physical awareness, and the importance of maintaining balance, strength, flexibility, and stamina.

The second part of the book, *How the Violin Plays the Mind*, focuses on cultivating mindfulness, awareness, objectivity and acceptance in the violinist's mind.

The third and final part, *Integrating the Violin with Our Entire Being*, includes ideas on how to effectively link all our active and interactive components, body-mind-spirit, by tapping into the resources within.

SUGGESTIONS FOR USING THIS BOOK

Even though this book focuses specifically on violin playing, much of the content can be applied to students, teachers and parents of students playing all instruments.

Read the book in order, or randomly flip through to any chapter of interest.

Text boxes (like this one) are hands-on project suggestions.

1

How the Violin Plays the Body

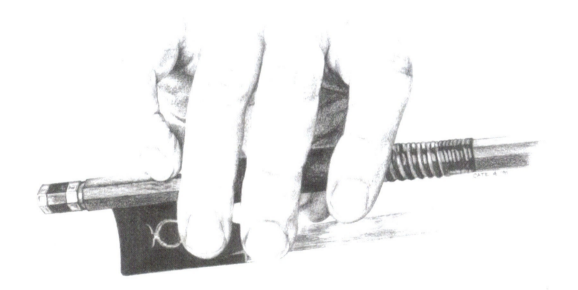

Beyond the body and mind,

sound touches

the spirit.

For those of us who choose the violin as the medium of our 'music play' there are specific considerations with regard to using our bodies. In *How the Violin Plays the Body*, I begin with an anatomical overview, followed by observations concerning the physical demands violin playing exerts on the body. This background then leads us further into an exploration of healthful attitudes in the body while playing. The subject of physical injury is introduced in this chapter, along with suggestions on how to release physical blocks to our creative flow.

Know Your Body

A general knowledge of body structure and how it works is invaluable to anyone who plays and teaches the violin. Violinists are small muscle athletes, requiring strentgh, agility, and fine motor coordination, particularly of the small muscle groups in the upper torso. Any music we play must travel through the medium of the body. So, it is important to begin with some very general information about anatomy, including visual reference charts.

> The **skeletal structure** is comprised of 206 bones. It supports the body's form, protects organs, and provides for the attachment of muscles to bones, allowing movement. (See diagram on page 7.)
>
> **Muscles** are the primary movers of the body, enabling the support of weight, and the performance of actions through contractions of muscle groups. (See diagrams on pages 8 and 9.)
>
> **Tendons** attach muscles to the bones.
>
> **Joints** form the connection between two or more bones. They are constructed to allow both simple and complex movement in our musculoskeletal structure and they provide mechanical support.
>
> **Ligaments** are fibrous tissues which connect bones or cartilage at a joint. Ligaments support and strengthen joints.

The body has three general **planes of motion**:

- ❖ the **sagittal plane** (lateral division of the right and left into symmetrical sides)

- ❖ the **frontal plane** (lateral division of the front/anterior and back/posterior halves)

- ❖ the **transverse plane** (horizontal division of upper and lower body).

The **diagonal or oblique plane** refers to the combination of more than one plane of motion.

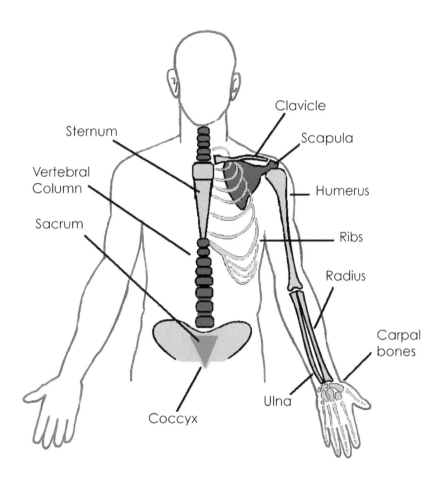

Skeletal System Chart

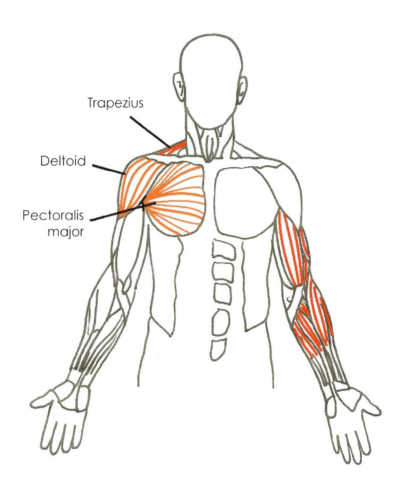

Muscle System Chart
Anterior View

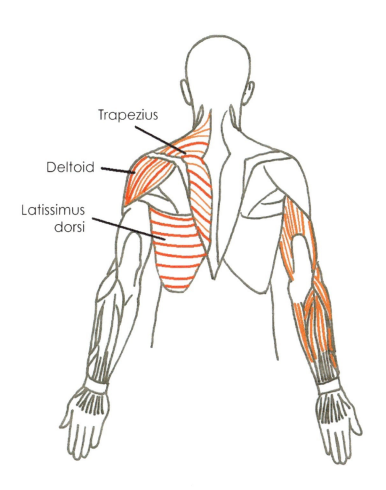

**Muscle System Chart
Posterior View**

Appreciate your brain's miraculous capacity to memorize habits and patterns. Performance reveals our mind and body practice habits with remarkable precision.

What the Violin Asks of the Player's Body

To support the body in a balanced, standing posture, many muscle groups, from the toes to the head, are at work. The violinist's body layers this with supporting the arms in front and somewhat to the sides of the body, with the hands above the heart – an action engaging the leg, core, back, neck, shoulder, and arm muscles. In playing position, supporting the bow and the weight of the violin is added, while many angles and directions of rotation also come into play in the neck, arms and hands. Once playing, the violinist really becomes involved in an athletic undertaking. All muscles and joints in the upper body fluctuate through simple and complex motions, being activated and/or relaxed.

Observing a violinist in a ready-to-play stance, with the instrument in their hands, one can clearly see **asymmetry** in the demands made on **each side of the upper body** (sagittal plane of motion) as well as in **the front and back of the upper body** (frontal plane). While much of this asymmetry is dissipated once the violinist begins playing, it is nevertheless important to consider the most obvious of these imbalances, for they are at the root of most common injuries related to playing the violin.

Observing how a violinist uses the torso and neck

- ❖ When playing, a violinist actively uses his or her arms in the frontal and sagittal planes of the body (never behind the back), thereby contracting frontal torso and arm muscles, while extending back torso muscles. (See photo below.)

- ❖ The head, neck and spine pass through constant, subtle adjustments while playing. Generally, the head rotates toward the violin to the left, not to the right. (See photo below.)

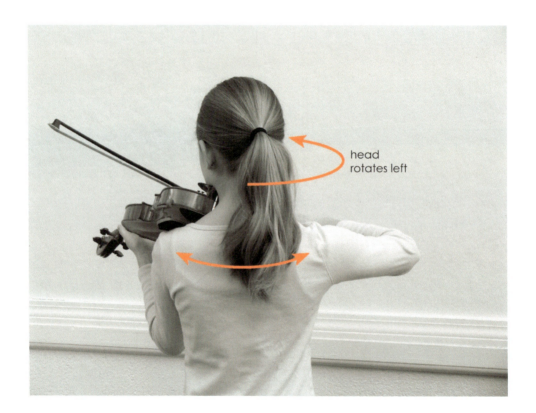

- ❖ Any over-rotation of the head toward the left, or clamping of the instrument between the jaw and shoulder, causes the left front neck muscles to contract, and the right side and back neck muscles to extend.

The left latissimus dorsi, pectoralis, trapezius, upper and forearm muscles are constantly engaged carrying weight and maintaining a horizontal position of the violin between the shoulder and left hand. When actively playing, rotations from the shoulder guide the hand to different strings and to higher or lower positions. Extensions and contractions in the left upper arm and forearm (horizontally away from or toward the left shoulder) allow us to balance the hand frame, to shift to different positions, and to use arm vibrato.

Shaded area indicates engaged left side torso and arm muscles.

❖ Muscles on the left side are **relatively** immobile compared with the right pectoralis, shoulder, and arm muscles, which, depending on string level and the part of bow, have a far more varied and extensive range of motion. The right side also has the advantage of being able to make use of gravity, pulling the bow into the string. Once in action, the bow continues to be balanced in the arm, hand, and fingers, and for certain bow strokes, the stick is lifted or carried. Specific bow strokes, variations in speed and strength of tone, allow the right side to be in constant, dynamic motion.

Shaded areas indicate engaged muscles.
The line on the player's bow arm (right arm) indicates engaged top muscles.

- ❖ While the left forearm is primarily engaged in supination (seen in the rotation of the forearm from the elbow, palm toward the neck of the violin), the bow arm is able to pronate (from the player's view – counterclockwise rotation of the forearm) *and* supinate (clockwise rotation of the forearm). **Note:** the amount of supination in the bow arm is dependant upon specific bow strokes and upon the general teaching approach.

Arrows indicate directions of pronation and supination.

By listening to what the body tells us it needs, and by heeding that message, it is not only possible to prevent injury, but also to recover from injury.

Discovering and Maintaining Balance in the Violinist's Body

Physical health as a violinist can be maintained and sustained through regular physical exercise *apart* from the instrument, paired with an awareness of how the body feels *while* playing the violin. Through activities like walking, running, swimming, playing tennis, or practicing yoga, one can release pent-up energy, clear the mind, and receive new energy.

Developing awareness of our body as we play our instrument implies listening to what the body tells us it needs, and heeding that message. By respecting our body in this way, it is not only possible to prevent injury, but also to recover from injury. This awareness also greatly benefits our well being – body, mind, and spirit.

This section provides general ideas on how to best use the musculoskeletal system (the skeletal system, muscular system and joints) when we play. Also throughout this section are references to the application of universal principles of balance, symmetry, gravity, the flow of energy, and laws of motion as they relate to playing.

Educational Kinesiology® (also known as Brain Gym®) describes brain functioning in three dimensions:

- side to side
- front to back
- top to bottom

This corresponding relationship also exists in the body and its planes of motion:

- left side to right side
- front to back
- upper half to lower half

By balancing these dimensions in the body, one improves the efficiency, flow, and functioning of both the brain AND the body!

Healthy use of the musculoskeletal system

Imagine being able to see your skeletal structure while holding and playing the violin. Through movement and action, the body is constantly adjusting the various balances between the top and bottom of the body, side to side, and front to back.

The most beneficial ways of using the musculoskeletal system include:

- balancing from the hips upward and downward

- knowing that the heaviest part of the body (the head) is at the top of the skeletal system

- being aware that the spine meets the head in the center of the neck between the ears (balance the head by using the spine and neck region as if you were a living "bobble head")

- allowing the spine's natural alignment, curvature, and free movement (be aware of any rigidity, holding, unnatural twisting or angles in the spinal vertebrae)

- tilting the sacrum slightly forward

- opening the shoulders back (imagine bringing the scapulae toward each other, while lifting the sternum)

- keeping the left and right shoulders horizontally aligned

- feeling the rib cage expanding the opening, instead of slumping or collapsing

Healthy use of muscles

It is of key importance when playing an instrument like the violin, that muscles not specifically engaged in actions be "turned off," or allowed to relax whenever possible.

> ❖ An awareness of what activated and relaxed muscles feel like can be introduced to very young players by exploring the feeling of **opposites**:
>
> Be as tight, rigid and "squeezy" as you can.
> Now release and move like a jellyfish...let go!
>
> This can be done using either the whole body,
> or more specifically, the bow hold or left hand.
>
> ❖ As sensitivity develops, one can direct a player's attention to **levels of intensity** graduated on a scale of 1 to 10 (1 being the softest or gentlest, building towards 10, which is maximum power).

Healthy Joints

For a violinist, healthy joints have a feeling of softness or flexibility about them while supporting the form. Rigidity in the joints (bending, stiffness, curling, angular shapes, and/or locking) creates blocks preventing the flow of energy through the body.

> Awareness of the joints can be introduced when setting up a balanced body posture for beginners:
>
> - Place feet hip-width apart.
> - To feel the feet resting fully on the floor, roll both feet to the right, then to the left; lean weight into the toes, then into the heels. Finally, come to rest noticing the feeling of the "4 corners" of the feet in contact with the floor. Open the toes slightly.
> - Next, feel where the ankles are (circular motion/lift and drop heels).
> - Soft knee joints are stacked above the ankles.
> - Hips above ankles and knees.
> - Shoulders aligned above ankles, knees and hips (see diagram on page 22).
> - To finish, check the top of the spine using a gentle "bobble head" motion.

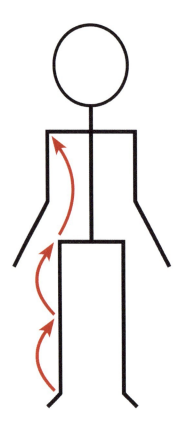

In a well balanced set-up, flexible joints (ankles, knees, hips and shoulders) are vertically aligned.

It is useful for a violinist to realize that the upper and lower body joints (transverse plane of motion) have a relationship to each other: shoulders to hips, elbows to knees, wrists to ankles.

There also is a cross relationship side to side (oblique plane of motion):

- ❖ shoulders to hips (diagram a)
- ❖ elbows to knees (diagram b)
- ❖ wrists to ankles (diagram c)

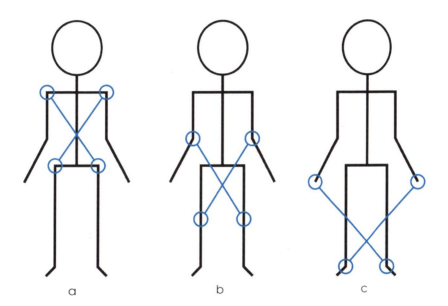

a   b   c

Two examples of how to apply this information to a violinist's body

Upper to lower body:
- locked shoulders can be released by initiating circular motion in the hips

Side to side:
- A tight left wrist can be released by loosening the right ankle

As already stated, when a player engages in the use of extreme angles, locking, or tightening of the joints, one creates blocks which prevent the flow of energy. Any joint used in this way taxes numerous muscle groups as well. For example, intentionally locking the left wrist joint causes a contagious, locking chain reaction in the other joints of the arm (elbow, shoulder, and fingers).

Conversely, by consciously releasing one joint set in the arm, the chain reaction occurs again, this time transferring a supple, loose, and flexible feeling to all joints. Even breathing becomes easier. This kind of letting go in the core of the joints allows a healthy channel of energy flow from the feet and legs, through the core, torso, arms, hands and fingers. This energy flow can then emerge through the instrument. The free sensation for the player and the resultant tone says it all.

Lines indicate free flow of energy when joints are supple and loose.

One of the best practice methods to assure that the joints release for clear energy paths is to play the violin sitting on an **exercise ball** (feet flat on the floor, thighs parallel to floor, spine upright).

Other advantages of playing while sitting on an exercise ball

For the mind:

- Exercise balls can stimulate a healthy sense of playfulness.

For the brain:

- Using an exercise ball can enliven alertness AND/OR it can induce calmness.
- The brain becomes largely engaged in directing the physical act of balancing. This causes any playing to move into the subconscious realm, ultimately revealing the level of competence and integration of the work at hand.

For the body:

- Joints and muscles learn to respond to an unstable environment.
- Core strength, balance, and coordination improve.
- Posture is improved as the spine releases downward with gravity and is also reminded of the habit of lengthening.
- Flexibility is improved.
- Breathing is stimulated.

Allow swinging motion in left shoulder

Most, if not all, violinists know the feeling of a frozen left shoulder (involving the pectoralis and trapezius). To counteract this condition, it is healthy to develop a habit of frequently swinging the left arm under the violin before playing, while playing (when possible), and after playing.

> Without the instrument in hand, stand with the feet hip-width apart, and do a simple windmill – rotating hips, shoulders and floppy arms in a circular motion from side to side.

Energy, weight, and gravity transferred through the right arm and bow, are counterbalanced by the left shoulder shelf, the string, and left thumb energy.

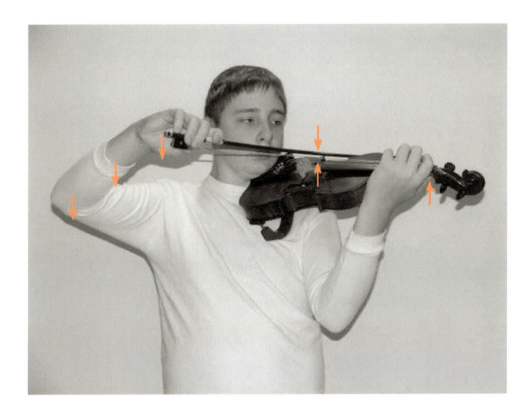

A violinist can become aware of, and make use of the exchange of energy in upward and downward vertical relationships, or systems of balance – violin to bow, left arm to right arm, instrument to body, and body to instrument. This kinesthetic feeling and understanding can in turn lead to an excellent sensation of release and flow of focused energy. Another result of this relationship is the feeling that the violin and bow live in a neutral, horizontal plane. The effects on tone production are outstanding.

> **Newton's Third Law of Motion:**
> For every action, there is an equal and opposite reaction.

Allow active and reactive motion. A habit of holding or freezing reactive motion can lead to injury.

Reestablishing balance through yogic stretches and postures

Many musicians have found the practice of yoga beneficial for calmness and clarity in the mind, as well as for healing, strengthening, and rejuvenating the body. Consider the following yogic principle: **for every asana (pose), there is a counter asana which re-establishes harmony and balance to the entire system.**

One can apply this principle to a violinist's body by practicing stretches and strengthening postures which stimulate use of the body in directions and actions equal and opposite to the predominate use while playing.

For example:

- **To bring relief to the neck:**

    Keeping the chin parallel to the floor, inhale. While rotating the head on the spine slowly to the right, exhale. Inhale back to center. Exhale while rotating the head on the spine to the left. Inhale back to center. Repeat.

- **To stretch and release the larger torso and arm muscles:**

    Drop the chin to the chest. Clasp the hands in a finger-lock behind the back. Exhale. On the inhale, slowly bring the head up. Open the chest and stretch the arms by extending the hands toward the heels. Bring shoulder blades toward each other. Hold. Exhale while slowly dropping the chin to the chest. Continue to clasp hands while relaxing the arms. Repeat with the breath.

- **To rebalance the extreme supination of the left arm:**

    Hold the arms extended in front of the body or to the sides just below the shoulder level. Slowly rotate both arms in clockwise and counter-clockwise directions. Breathe!

Physical Injury

The causes of physical injury in violinists are most often rooted in the misuse of their bodies, destructive attitudes in the mind, or combinations of both.

As a sensitive artist, a musician's self-perception, self-esteem, and confidence in their abilities are profoundly influenced and conditioned by the words and actions of their teachers, mentors, and conductors. An approach of "only one correct way" and harsh criticism necessitates a player's development of resiliency or thick skin, and can cause blocks and/or tension in the body (which may eventually lead to injury). A nurturing approach can teach a player to be receptive and open, accepting and at ease in their body.

Many serious students and professionals play in competitive environments, practicing long hours, often under anxious, stressful conditions. While some players thrive in competitive settings, sustaining a high level of excellence under prolonged pressure or with urgency can be wearing on our systems. Constantly pushing to the edge may be thrilling, but over time it can lead to a burn-out or breakdown in the body, mind, or spirit.

Musicians invite injuries through mindless repetition, practicing without taking notice of being tired in their arms or minds, or pushing through practices without taking frequent breaks. Initial hints of misuse may be subtle (e.g., discomfort through overextending or overrotating muscles and joints; using muscles in a way that causes them to spasm or become hardened; tension headaches in the shoulders or neck). In time, these imbalances can compound, leading to more serious injuries including: tinnitus, tendonitis, carpal tunnel syndrome, rotator cuff injuries, and severe nerve injuries. These physical blocks can take weeks, months, or even years to be released and rebalanced, or before they pass through the system.

Acute and chronic conditions can become debilitating to the point where we become unable to function (can't practice; can't perform; can't teach). In such cases, it is no longer possible to avoid or ignore the symptoms or the causes of them. Lasting recovery cannot begin until we take the time to give ourselves the necessary nurturing, rest, and space for healing, or perhaps to even revolutionize our mind and physical approach. Without these steps, it is likely we will continue to remain stuck.

The following story relates one of my own experiences with work-related injuries and recovery.

The Practice of Yoga

It was not until I was in graduate school, that the anxiety I regularly carried inside about not being good enough, paired with tension headaches and extreme tightness in my shoulders, really began to get in my way. I remember days when I would cancel rehearsals or teaching to lie on my back with my neck resting on a bag of hot boiled potatoes (an old folk remedy recommended by my doctor in Germany). And so it went on until a few years later, when I was back in the United States, I developed ringing in my left ear, hyperacusis (sound sensitivity), and a loss of low frequency hearing. My initial response was one of panic. I was fearful and anxious that perhaps this was "the beginning of the end" of my career as a violinist. Desperation began to creep in as I tried to control and monitor every note I played and heard. I questioned my accuracy, inspecting everything, as it were, with a magnifying glass. Soon, confidence in my abilities started to dwindle. I embarked on a frenzy of tests and visits to specialists. Then, after trying everything western medicine could offer to no avail, I finally heeded a friend's recommendation, and went to my first yoga class.

My introduction to the practice of yoga – life journey toward a union of body, mind, and spirit – was a profound turning point in my personal and professional existence. Not only did this practice aid my physical healing, it also helped me reconnect and integrate with my whole self. Yoga provided a philosophy and way of viewing life which has forever transformed my whole person. In time, I was able to fully recover and return to the violin playing and teaching that I love.

In hindsight, this experience with physical injury taught me the futility of being tough on my body, and of being harshly self-critical in my mind. I had to essentially rewire my patterns of reaction. Dread in the face of discomfort, illness and injury was replaced with attitudes of acceptance and being open to opportunities for growth. My true healing and recovery began, not when I fueled cycles of negativity, but when I was able to come into states of objectivity through acceptance. I acknowledged the discomfort or pain, but instead of wasting energy wishing it away, I learned to accept and let it be there. The discomfort lasted until I began to understand the message the imbalance gave me. In time, the injury moved out of my system, and I returned fully healed.

In conclusion, the single most important message contained in this chapter, lies in the value of the **individual violinist coming to know and understand their body well**: to be aware of how the body is structured; to recognize what postures the instrument requires the player to maintain and sustain; and which parts of their structure or moving systems are activated by playing. The more awareness we have of these principles, the less likely we are to become injured. AND the more awareness we have, the more efficiently the body will function as the medium through which our music is transferred through the instrument to our audience.

You are the master of the

moments of your life.

Paramahansa Yogananda

2

How the Violin Plays the Mind

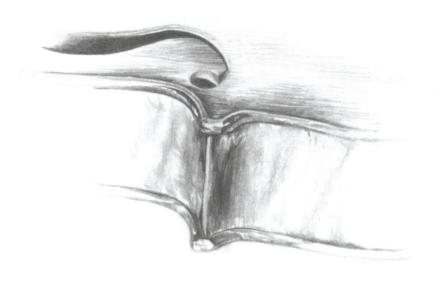

Music played at a given moment in time can never be reproduced – it lives only in that moment.

While there are physical implications of playing which effect a player's mind (tension, discomfort, injury, ease), so the mind can effect the functioning of a player's body (anxiety, fear, calmness, alertness).

In this chapter, *How the Violin Plays the Mind*, I explore constructive methods of directing the mind, for the benefit of our expression through music.

Awareness opens the door to calm, gentle responses toward ourselves, those around us, and to all experiences.

Awareness

Awareness is **the ability to notice** or **observe the present moment**. It is an alertness and attention to the energy of NOW. Present moment awareness encompasses all that surrounds us in our external environment (physical presence, all that enlivens the senses), AND it encompasses that which resides in our internal environment (thoughts, feelings in the body and mind, even stillness, spaciousness, and emptiness).

Young musicians come to an awareness of themselves through their instrument using their ears, their sense of touch, and their eyes. Players also develop an awareness of their part in the musical life around them each and every time they play with other musicians, be it an accompanist, an ensemble, or an orchestra.

Bringing awareness to our connection with and through the instrument occurs in a dynamic state, always changing. The ability to be curious, conscious, and aware in the present moment of everything that is occurring can provide freshness in our playing, a sense of fun, pleasure, and revelations which often lead to breakthroughs. Awareness is not judgment. It is simply being observant: calmly, objectively observant. Healthy awareness carries within it an acceptance of what we observe – "it is what it is." For example, a violinist may observe, without judgment, "my left fingers feel fluid and energetic" or "today I feel tired and sluggish." Fine – now I can play on, enjoying the sound and sensation of energy present in the fluid fingers, or I can gently coax the tired sluggish attitude in my mind and body toward alertness by stimulating aliveness in my playing (highlighting rhythmic precision, articulation, velocity, and fluency in body movements).

Awareness opens the door to calm, gentle responses toward ourselves, those around us, and to all experiences. It is devoid of the emotional charge of ego-driven reactions. Through awareness, we can learn to release our body and mind by letting go of all that is rigid, tight, and resistant. We can move away from the seriousness which stifles self-expression, into softness and playfulness.

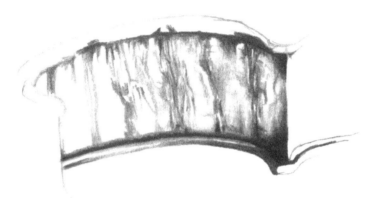

Objectivity

> Awareness leads to objectivity

It is important for musicians of all ages to know how to access and cultivate the habit of objectivity – **observation without judgment** or **awareness without personal attachment**. Objectivity opens the window to channeling (giving and receiving) music freely.

When we approach our instrument in a state of heightened emotion, expectations, urgency, or time pressure, we may in fact be setting ourselves up to experience frustration, judgment, and even fear. This state of being causes changes in breathing. The emotional charge also causes chemical changes in the body. A domino effect is set into motion, impacting clarity and efficiency of directions from the brain, as well as functioning of the nerves and the musculoskeletal structure. Ultimately these consequences can be heard and felt in our playing. We may then enter a state of judgment, and experience feelings of disappointment. All our systems begin to contract, and so we ride a downward spiral.

It is wise to establish a habit of checking in with ourselves before picking up the violin to practice, before taking a lesson, and certainly before walking on stage to give a performance. This method prepares all aspects of our being to be fully present. Checking in includes noticing our breathing (without judgment), noticing how we feel in our skin (without judgment), noticing if there are any emotions we are carrying (without judgment).

Calmness can be induced through conscious breathing, i.e., breathing with awareness. Breathing is the means whereby we connect our body-mind-spirit.

The next step is to be clear on what experience we invite. When practicing, one can **set goals that clarify what we want**; OR **approach a task in exploration mode** – discover what is there. Before a lesson, have it in mind to be available and open to all our teacher offers, ready to go for the ride!

The habits of mind-body approach, and habits of response which we reinforce in home practice and during lessons or coaching sessions, are what carry us when we walk on stage to perform. All we need do is to simply ask to be open and accepting of all that occurs in the present moment.

Acceptance and Allowance

Acceptance, not to be confused with resignation, goes hand in hand with a state of surrender or, as my British uncle would say, "giving over." It is the ability to remain open, **to be with things as they are** in a given moment. Often we have a wish to erase certain experiences, or to replay and change them, to take away pain or discomfort, to take back perceived mistakes. Yet it is through these very experiences that we grow. How different life would be if we were able to view these occurrences as opportunities for learning. Perhaps we could even go so far as to live with the habit of being at ease with and grateful for ALL experiences whether we register them as comfortable or uncomfortable.

If a mistake can be viewed, appreciated, and valued as a learning tool, then the experience has been the perfect lesson.

Mis-takes

I'll never forget the day when the mother of one of my students looked at me and said, "You mean, you allow your students to make mistakes?"

Many of us have been conditioned, as this mother was, to consider mistakes on a par with committing an offence – something to be avoided at all costs. Traditionally, mistakes are labels which we (or often our parents, teachers and conductors) issue anytime we experience or hear inaccuracy in our playing: imperfections, like a missed shift, an incorrect bowing, pitches which are out of tune, a garbled passage, or a memory blank. The negative energy behind a mistake label can make us feel ashamed and embarrassed because we have somehow failed to deliver. It can take us into a state of self-degradation or even anger. This attitude toward mistakes is destructive. It rarely brings improvement, and leads us further away from, instead of closer to, flawless performing.

Step back a moment. Consider re-viewing this word as "mis-take" or a "missed take." Do you feel a fresh energy of objectivity coming into play? Notice also that a "missed take" lives in the past. It is over! There is no value in attaching emotional energy or holding on to what has already occurred. This is not to say, however, that we should ignore the occurrence. Take notice of mis-takes and acknowledge them simply as parts of our playing which are "asking us to visit the next time we're in town" doing mindful practice. When mis-takes occur during performance, move your energy into the present moment, where you are actively engaged. Here you can lay the groundwork for what unfolds in the future.

> Sources of mis-takes are many and varied. A player's technical or musical challenge zones, and momentary distractions are what most often reveal themselves through mis-takes.

In our work as musicians, we can choose to face challenges head-on, or we can choose to avoid them for as long as possible. If ignored and left to grow wild, these challenges can eventually dominate our music. They deprive our playing of energies vital to sustaining growth, enjoyment of the learning process, and ultimately beauty. Avoidance does not make a challenge go away; and it can lead to negative associations with a composition, with our violin, or even with other people (our parents and teachers).

So what do we do with challenges revealed through mis-takes – the weeds in the garden of our music?

Firstly, **accept and acknowledge** the presence of technical or musical weeds. If they show up in the form of mis-takes, remember that these are non-intentional occurrences, provided for our learning process. **Mis-takes are always part of our learning process**.

Similar to caring for a garden, weed-like challenges in the form of mis-takes, are managed by literally **extracting one at a time. Simplify and breakdown** a challenge to its most basic components (weeds can have flowers, leaves, stems, and roots). Use **one point practice** or **one point focus** to eventually eradicate the whole weed. Superficially pulling the top off the weed (surface practice) does not necessarily extract the roots. Remember that roots can be shallow or deep. Stay with it, persist until the growth of your flawless playing strengthens and emerges.

Use **mindful repetitions**, or "be fully present with your mind" when practicing. Complexities of difficult passages in music are often compounded, reinforced, or practiced into a piece through mindless repetition. Mindless repetition is a clear invitation to mis-takes. Is that really what you want?

Practice challenging parts **meticulously, with calmness and clarity of purpose.** Mis-takes can reveal passages which have not yet been explored thoroughly enough to become familiar and fluent. Discover those passages, go directly to them, find out what they need to grow and blossom into beautiful plants. A litmus test for ease and readiness to perform is to notice any changes in your breathing or how your body feels when approaching and playing through intricate passages. Do you look forward to every part of your piece, or are you crossing your fingers hoping to get through it?

The habits of **being attentive in the present moment**, and **reinforcing one aspect of your playing at a time** in home practice, are what carry us in a performance. Lapses in concentration or momentary distractions (common causes of mis-takes) will become less frequent.

Practice noticing mis-takes, not reacting to them. For students, common reactions to mistakes may be:

- ❖ to quickly rewind and try a "re-take"
- ❖ to apologize to the world with "sorry"
- ❖ to swear!
- ❖ to go into facial antics

Appreciate your brain's miraculous capacity to memorize habits and patterns. Performance reveals our mind and body practice habits with remarkable precision. If your habit is to scowl for every out-of-tune pitch, the scowl literally becomes part of the composition (as if Mozart wrote it in the score). If your practiced habit is to hold up the "I made a mistake" sign every time one occurs, that is where your energy and attention will go. Instead, **practice developing the art of objectively accepting mis-takes.** Play through your piece with green lights all the way. Be in observation mode. Accept all aspects of your playing. Move away from verbal and physical manifestations of reactions to mis-takes.

Mentors, teachers and parents (like the mother of my student) have good intentions – they want their students and children to have experiences which feel good. Yet, what child, or for that matter what person of any age can learn without taking chances, without being **allowed** to fall and scrape their knees through mis-takes? In life, mis-takes happen! If a mis-take can be viewed, appreciated, and valued as a learning tool, then the experience has been the perfect lesson. It need not be an occurrence which causes us to cringe or become fearful.

To summarize, as a musician, I have come to learn that mis-takes are simply indicators which point to where our song or skill still needs to grow in familiarity and ease. It's as simple as that.

I have also learned as a musician, that pouring energy into trying to avoid mis-takes – cautiously tiptoeing our way through a practice or performance – can actually produce them!

So, what would it be like to be fully immersed in all aspects of the learning process? To reach a point of being grateful for the lessons brought through ALL experiences (including mis-takes) past, present and future? This is acceptance – a way of being which leads to a greater sense of fulfillment and freedom in all we do.

Intention

It is through both an innate sense, and exposure to beautiful tone, that we, players, are inspired to express our own relationship with tonal qualities and music as beautifully as we can. We establish an image or **intention** for our playing.

We hold the instrument in our hands poised to pull the violin's strings with our bow. **Action** is directed from the brain through the muscles, joints, and general body structure. We play.

Our mind has an extraordinary ability, at any given moment in time, to recall the past and notice the present, while projecting into the future. When we are playing our instrument, the brain receives and processes sensory, motor and emotional input in all three time frames simultaneously. We evaluate and compare the **resultant outcome** of our actions with the ideal in our mind.

This is followed by a **response**. How close was that to my ideal? Did I get what I wanted? Yes or no? Our teachers and other listeners also provide feedback.

It is both our personal response to the consequence of our action and the feedback from our listeners which guide us, if necessary, to reset the intention. If our initial intention is not manifested in the outcome, we can be more specific in restating our goal. Once we are able to produce the sound or effect that was intended, we then engage in conscious repetition to strengthen our ability to reproduce it. With practice, the sequencing becomes refined and reinforced, and in time, an easy subconscious flow emerges.

One can apply the following intention formula for efficient practice and growth.

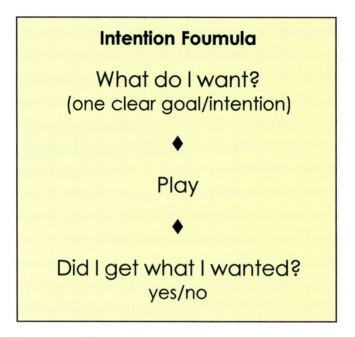

Reinforce "yes" (at least **three in a row** each practice) until there is ease. One can also refine the goal by being more specific as to qualities we may want.

If the outcome of our intention is predominantly "no" (we *did not* get what we wanted), simplify the goal/intention by breaking it down into more basic components. Verbally state/restate the goal each time. Play SLOWER. Stay with one basic component at a time, until "yes" predominates in our playing (at least **three in a row** each practice); then and only then are we ready to add the next layer in the form of a new goal/intention.

Note: This is a clever method for efficient practice and for stimulating independence in practice. While initial guidance from the teacher or parent on how to use this system is important, it only truly becomes effective for the player if they are clearly aware of their intention, and once they learn to recognize, identify, and verbalize whether they achieved what they wanted.

I conclude the present chapter, *How the Violin Plays the Mind,* with a short story based on an experience I had as a teacher (modified where necessary to protect the student's privacy).

Janie Invites a Mess-up!

Twelve year-old Janie soloed at my spring student recital. She had known her piece for many months, and had spent the last weeks leading up to the performance incorporating finishing touches. She was ready to go.

Janie's moment arrived in the program. She got up, balanced well, started her piece, and was having a strong run. No one would have known this was a shy teenager who worked with me each week for up to 10 minutes on tone and projection routines before she would REALLY play the violin.

Nearing the end of a beautiful presentation, Janie was suddenly stopped by what appeared to be a memory lapse. She couldn't hear the piano cues, she grinned, and she clicked her tongue. The audience sat in silence, sending an encouraging wave of energy through the room, helping Janie to move forward. And so she did. The final bow was accompanied by a downcast, disappointed look. She left the stage and went to sit near her parents, where she likely got some hugs, and had a few tears.

Since I didn't see Janie after the recital, I telephoned later to check in. Her mother answered and said her daughter was "devastated." (I suspect the mother may have been speaking for herself!) I spoke to Janie, reminding her of the fine example she had provided of solid tone (yeah!), phrasing, and of all the hundreds of notes she had strung together beautifully and well. I also complimented her on the courage and perseverance she had demonstrated to everyone, by standing there and seeing it through to the end.

In Janie's next lesson, I asked how she was doing. She gave her little grin and said, "fine." "So, Janie," I asked, "is there anything you could have done to have been better prepared?" She took a moment then answered, "No." "Do you have any recollection of what was going through your mind at that point in the performance?" I asked. She quickly answered, "Oh, yeah, from my first note I was thinking don't mess up, don't mess up, don't mess up."

In the light of this answer, I think Janie's experience was a perfect example of a phenomenon she and others can learn from.

Energy follows intention. Like the principle of sympathetic vibration, the energy we send out will resonate with and be answered by whatever physical objects (or even states of mind) are on a similar frequency. By focusing our attention on what we want, we invite what we want into our experience, AND by focusing our attention on what we don't want, we invite what we don't want into our experience.

Therefore, in order to attract whatever it is we want into our lives, we have to be clearly aware of how and where we direct the energy behind our intentions, which then effects change in our feelings, alters the frequency of our vibrations, and ultimately attracts what we most want into our experience.

Contrast is healthy! To identify what we do want, we need to know what we don't want.

3

Integrating the Violin with Our Entire Being

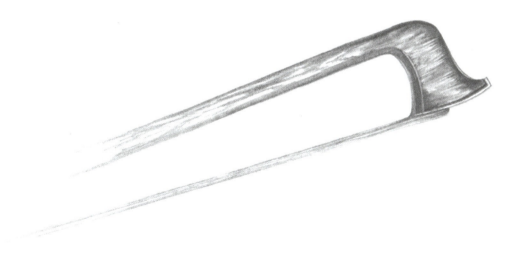

Our journey with a given composition unfolds and blossoms through the pragmatic study of and personal familiarity with the piece in our body, mind, and spirit.

The intention of this book is to explore how playing the violin informs the artist-musician's whole being. To a certain extent, it has been possible to distinguish or separate the roles of the body, mind and spirit – our body can be trained, our mind has rationality and freedom of choice, and our spirit flows in and expresses itself through both the body and mind.

Recognize though, that as soon as a player engages in action, these three aspects of our person (body, mind, and spirit) immediately flow, interact and play into one another becoming a beautiful inseparable unit. The ability to synchronize our whole being, and to transfer that oneness through our instrument, is at the heart of truly meaningful performance.

The purpose of this final chapter is to be reminded of our inner resources, through which it is possible to more fully integrate the playing of the violin with our whole being.

Home is where the heart is –
bringing the easiness of home,
and feeling the presence of our
heart in all we do.

Tapping Into the Resources Within

Home is where the heart is

As violinists and teachers, how often have we found ourselves thinking, or heard our students commenting, "it was easier at home" or "I don't know what's happening. It sounded great at home?" What changes take place between home practice, and the playing we do at a lesson, at exams, or when we walk on stage to perform?

In a physical sense, the biggest differences seem to lie in environmental and acoustic changes. For the mind, the most obvious change is our perception of the audience as we step outside of the home comfort zone. In our desire to show or play our best, we may find that we use more effort. Perhaps we become acutely aware of details, while other sounds and movements in the room may become magnified, distracting us. We may even experience elements of the "fight or flight" response. There are suddenly **many** new ears in the room. We play knowing and expecting some form of reaction or commentary when our piece has ended – feedback which we may receive as criticism and judgment rather than constructive input. As we aspire to match and play the perfection we hear in our inner song, many musicians even find the art of absorbing and accepting compliments challenging. We know our desire is to perform to the best of our ability, from the heart, yet simultaneously we may find ourselves treading carefully, breathing cautiously, steeling ourselves against feedback, with some of the harshest critique likely coming from ourselves!

Why is all this necessary when all we really wanted was to play beautifully? Why can't we be playing with the comfort and ease we know is possible?

> How can we bring that feeling of "home is where the heart is" into all we're doing right here, right now?
> - ❖ by being aware of what intention(s) we are giving fuel or energy to in a given moment
> - ❖ by acknowledging where we are in the process of making a piece our own

What intention are we giving fuel or energy to? As stated in the previous chapter, **energy follows intention** or **intention directs attention**. In preparation for performance and during performance, what are the most beneficial intentions one can choose? Where specifically can we focus our attention in order to reach states of comfort and ease in performance? In my experience, feeling at home in my heart while performing has been most successfully accessed by choosing to engage in one of three fundamental intentions:

- ❖ **listening**, and accepting what I hear
- ❖ **feeling**, and accepting what I feel
- ❖ **breathing**, noticing and/or engaging in deep, full breathing

Where are we in the process of making a piece our own? Our journey with a given composition unfolds and blossoms through the pragmatic study of and personal familiarity with the piece in our body, mind, and spirit. **Owning a piece** allows one to play freely from the heart.

What are the building blocks to making a piece our own?

- ❖ Understanding, constantly refining and being able to accurately execute **technical skills or passages** in a piece to the point of ease and integration.

- ❖ Researching and practicing one's ability to demonstrate **compositional elements** (rhythm in the context of beat, pitch accuracy, melody, harmony, form) and **musical elements** (bowing, phrasing, articulation, tone, vibrato, dynamics, personal nuance, expression).

- ❖ **Being able to sing our song** (literally with our outer and inner singing voice); knowing the whole composition in our ears and in the context of its setting – concerto, sonata, quartet.

- ❖ Being familiar with the piece to the point of **memorization.**

- ❖ **Allowing imagination and creativity to lead our playing** (for example, colors, textures, images, stories, stirring of emotions, associations with the composer's life, a time in history).

- ❖ Noticing if our **eyes** are able to be relaxed, blink, or even able to be closed when we play – this indicates that we are moving beyond needing the left brain to consciously direct actions.

- ❖ Reaching states in which our **body can move with fluency, coordination and balance**, devoid of anything angular or rigid.

- ❖ **Breathing** fully, deeply, and uninhibited.

Our central task as performers is to present an accurate interpretation of a given composer's work – and to do so with beauty and ease. Ideally we enter a zone where we are calmly alert, physically and mentally fluent, and available to unify our voice (through the instrument) with that of the orchestra or piano. We can also learn to appreciate (instead of dreading) the thrilling edge which comes from stepping outside the comfortable and familiar. It is possible to learn, create, and carry with us an underlying confidence that our home in the heart is right here with us. By truly immersing ourselves in this feeling, fear and aloneness dissipate, and we can find the freedom and inner calmness to be a truly content and competent performer.

> Remember – **listen, feel, breathe, and accept!**

Breathing

A key to accessing "home is where the heart is" – to be truly present with all one's love and connected to all sources from which love flows to us at any moment in time – lies in a resource so basic that we often forget we have it: our breathing!

In a metaphysical sense, breath is what UNIFIES our BEING – body, mind, and spirit.

Breathing is a **physical** and **emotional barometer**. Any change in our physical breathing, directly effects a change in our heart rate and brain functions, and *vice versa*. Thoughts and emotional reactions to situations can alter our breathing. Conversely, breathing with awareness can change our thoughts and emotional reactions.

Inhalations and exhalations can be objectively observed (notice your breathing when resting, listening, playing your instrument, performing); OR they can be actively engaged, for example, through the practice of various yogic breaths (described at the end of this section).

Breathing is also a **vital and integral part of all music**. Any convincing or moving interpretation of song (including the basic components of pulse, tone, intonation, phrasing, and for string players, bowing) is fully supported by our breathing.

Singers, as well as players of wind and brass instruments, know that music is only possible through developing, controlling and integrating the flow of air through their bodies and instruments. In contrast, string instrument players, pianists, and percussionists may initially be less connected to the power, vitality and effect which deep inhalation and exhalation can exert on their playing.

Interpreters of music benefit from specific training and guidance to understand, appreciate, and develop breathing habits which give life to their song. If we breathe consciously, our body softens, our power source from the solar plexus (the energy center below our ribs) opens, our voice (through the instrument) becomes clearer, and our ears seem to grow in alertness. The resultant effect is that our music breathes. A musician breathing freely through his or her playing also invites the listening audience to experience the ease and expressive feeling of life as it breathes through music.

Choosing to breathe fully and deeply, invites:

- ❖ calmness
- ❖ openness
- ❖ states of complete acceptance
- ❖ the ability to be fully present
- ❖ clear attention and intention
- ❖ feeling grounded
- ❖ creativity
- ❖ receptivity
- ❖ awareness without judgment
- ❖ emotional communication

In contrast, how do we feel when we hold our breath, or engage only in shallow breathing at the top of the rib cage? We may feel resistance, restriction, limited, shut down, small, unworthy, incompetent, frustrated, angry.

BREATHING EXERCISES

Conscious breathing can be practiced either in an upright seated position, or lying on your back, feet on the floor, knees in an A-frame shape. Notice that the vertebrae in the spine are aligned, and that no tension is being held in the head-neck region, arms, or legs. The belly is "open," i.e., soft, and relaxed.

Bhastrika (or bellows)
This breath feels like blowing out a birthday candle through the nose. Each rapid exhalation is followed by an immediate inhalation. This breath is particularly energetic in the region of the belly-button. Practice this breath for one minute – return to expansive breathing for one minute – repeat.

Benefits include: releasing carbon dioxide from the entire system, stimulating alertness in the brain, releasing tension, and oxygenating the entire system (this breath is particularly helpful before a performance if you are experiencing any hint of performance anxiety).

Expansive belly breath
This is a counted breath, which stimulates a feeling of connectedness in the body-mind-spirit. It also brings a state of calmness and acceptance to the mind. If lying down, gently place your hands on the lower belly. Inhale on a count of six – hold one count – exhale on a count of eight – hold two counts – repeat. On the inhalation, dare to let the belly fill and be as expansive as possible. On the exhalation, release all air until it feels as if the belly button will touch the spine. Continue for 10 minutes.

A player's inner singing voice expressed through their music is what attracts, resonates and connects our spirit with a listener's spirit.

Playing from Our Inner Song

Mastery of the violin is a lifelong quest – a journey which includes cycles of thrill and bliss juxtaposed with intense challenge. Those called to play the violin, are driven to persist by a deep abiding passion; a passion strong enough to outweigh any obstacles they might encounter; a longing and loving to express their inner song.

The **inner voice** expresses itself in two ways: with words (a largely left hemisphere brain activity) OR it expresses itself through the singing of songs without words (right hemisphere brain activity). The **language based** or **chattering inner voice** directs our actions, aids us with analysis, focuses on details, timing and sequence. It is the seat of the "I" and "me," the ego. The **singing inner voice** carries the perfect image of our music play. It paints the ideal picture. It guides present moment feeling and creativity in our playing – shape, color, beauty of tone, phrase, breathing and flow. The singing inner voice clarifies our musical intentions. It is the realm of connection and oneness with all. It is a limitless, precious, and very personal entity. The inner singing voice is the sound or song of our spirit, our inmost loves, our essence.

Playing from the inner song implies willingness to access, nurture and release the song of our spirit. Sharing on this level requires trust, honesty and dares us to be vulnerable. The gift in return – the singing of the inner voice fills and refills us with the supreme motivation and inspiration for playing!

I often think back to a principle imparted to me by my first teacher – **to play by heart**. As a child, I simply interpreted this to mean knowing my piece well enough to be able to play it from memory. Playing by heart, though, goes further. It extends beyond physical ease, comfort, integration and a thorough understanding of the composition. Playing by heart involves familiarity to the point of entering quietness in the mind and openness to the present moment. Once we reach these states, playing by heart allows us to access our music from our core, our heart. The inner singing voice emerges and can be freely expressed and heard through the channels of our mind, body and violin.

In the play of music, there is energy in the silence of a community of listeners. There is aliveness and subtlety in the connection through non-verbal communication. We can't see sound or hold it in our hands. Music played at a given moment in time can never be reproduced – it lives only in that moment.

Consider the extraordinary power in the release and blend of sounds from our instruments. It can transform emotions. It can transport us beyond the framework of time and space. A player's inner singing voice expressed through their music is what attracts, resonates and connects our spirit with a listener's spirit.

The resources we can access from within – the feeling heart and our breathing – never leave us as long as we live. Be present and accepting of how you feel at any given moment. Develop awareness of your breathing. In return, the physical body, the functioning of the brain, and thoughts in the mind, can become calm, clear, and alert. These resources are present with us always and available to us whenever we choose to call on them. These are the keys which open the door for us to play by heart, to allow our inner singing voice to flow uninhibited through our violin.

Conclusion

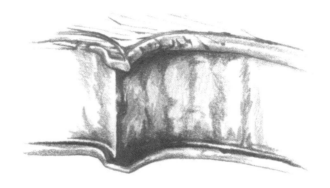

The ability to synchronize our whole being, and to transfer that oneness through our instrument, is at the heart of truly meaningful performance.

Play. What does it really mean to play one's instrument? Play is the love of expression and communication through sound. Play lies in the sensation of drawing the bow across the string. We are moved to play by emotions stirred when exploring works of certain composers. Play can celebrate the results which come from applying one's self and attaining specific musical goals. Play also hides itself within the challenges of striving toward mastery of the instrument.

The quest to play begins with the development of technical skills and the coordination of the brain and body with the instrument – the physical means through which we come to reveal our stories, our tone, or our expression living in the heart and mind. While much of the success of this quest to play lies in our commitment to excellence through practice, it must always be paired with the pursuit of ease and easiness in all we do, body, mind, and spirit. This adventurous process stretches us, and asks us to make discoveries about our whole being. So, how do we reach states of musical flow, freedom, and unity in all our systems? By allowing the violin to teach us; **by allowing the violin to play the violinist.**

It is my hope that this book has served as a source of ideas, concepts, and possibilities to consider, perhaps even generating some fresh curiosity. The definitive test for any philosophy or conceptual approach is to "see how the shoe fits" the individual – how does it sit with, sound, or feel to the player, or the listener? If we like the outcome, then we have the opportunity to incorporate and integrate, and continue the sharing cycle of what works for us with others. If the approach does not produce a favorable result, then we have lost nothing by trying. Personal freedom and choice are important, and it is through the gathering of knowledge that such choices are made apparent and available. Ultimately we all discover our own best path.

With these thoughts in mind, I wish you all happy playing!

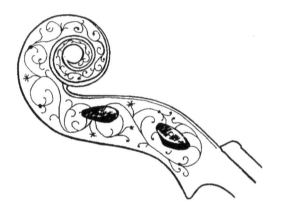

For comments, questions, or to order
more books, contact the author at
chowardsasc@gmail.com
OR
go to violinistbook.com

Sources

Casals, Pablo (as told to Kahn, Albert E.), *Joys and Sorrows*. New York, NY: Simon and Schuster, 1970.

Chödrön, Pema, *The Wisdom of No Escape*. Boston, MA: Shambahla Publications, Inc., 1991.

Conable, Barbara and Conable, Benjamin J., *What Every Musician Needs to Know About the Body, Revised Edition*. Portland, OR: Andover Press, 2000.

Dennison, Paul E., Ph.D. and Dennison, Gail E., *Brian Gym® Handbook, Second Edition*. Ventura, CA: Edu-Kinesthetics, Inc.

Desikachar, T.K.V., *The Heart of Yoga – Developing a Personal Practice, Revised Edition*. Rochester, VT: Inner Traditions International, 1999.

Flesch, Carl, *The Memoirs of Carl Flesch*. London, England: Da Capo Press (reprint of of 1957 ed. published by Rockliff), 1873-1944.

Grabhorn, Lynn, *Excuse Me, Your Life is Waiting*. Charlottesville, VA: Hampton Roads Publishing Company, Inc., 2000.

Gallwey, Timothy W., *The Inner Game of Tennis*. New York, NY: Random House, 1974.

Havas, Kato, *A New Approach to Violin Playing, Fourteenth Impression*. London, England: Bosworth & Co. Ltd., 2001.

Havas, Kato, *Stage Fright – Its Causes and Cures, Tenth Impression*. London, England: Bosworth & Co. Ltd., 1995.

Kabat-Zinn, Jon, *Wherever You Go There You Are*. New York, NY: Hyperion, 1994.

Kaplan, Burton, *Practicing for Artistic Success*. Morris, NY: Perception Development Techniques, 2004.

Kempter, Susan, *How Muscles Learn, Teaching the Violin with the Body in Mind*. Miami, FL: Summy-Birchard Inc., 2003.

Lieberman, Julie Lyonn, *You Are Your Instrument*. New York, NY: Huiksi Music, 1991.

Madder, Sylvia S., *Understanding Human Anatomy & Physiology, Fourth Edition*. New York, NY: McGraw-Hill, 2001.

Menuhin, Yehudi, *Unfinished Journey*. London, England: Macdonald and Jane's Publishers, 1976.

Morrison, Judith H., *The Book of Ayurveda, A Holistic Approach to Health and Longevity.* New York, NY: Fireside Simon & Schuster Inc., 1995.

Mozart, Leopold, (translated by Editha Knocker), *A Treatise on the Fundamental Principles of Violin Playing.* London, England: Oxford University Press, 1756-1948.

O'Brien, Dominic, *Learn to Remember.* London, England: Duncan Baird Publishers Ltd., 2000.

Restak, Richard, MD, *Mozart's Brain and the Fighter Pilot, Unleashing Your Brain's Potential.* New York, NY: Three Rivers Press, 2001.

Ristad, Eloise, *A Soprano on Her Head.* Moab, UT: Real People Press, 1982.

Schwartz, Boris, *Great Masters of the Violin.* New York, NY: Simon & Schuster, 1983.

Sher, Gail, *One Continuous Mistake, Four Noble Truths for Writers.* New York, NY: Penguin Group Penguin Putnam Inc., 1999.

Solomon, Alan, *Why Are You So Nervous? The Anatomy of Stage-Fright.* Johannesburg, South Africa: Taliesin Editions.

Stern, Isaac and Potok, Chaim, *Isaac Stern, My First 79 Years.* New York, NY: Alfred A. Knopf, 1999.

Suzuki, Shinichi, *Nurtured by Love.* Secaucus, NJ: Suzuki Method International Summy-Birchard Inc., 1983.

Swedenborg, Emanuel, Treatise on *Mechanical Tremulation, Vibration in the Body,* 1719.

Taylor, Jill Bolte, Ph.D., *My Stroke of Insight, A Brain Scientist's Personal Journey.* New York, NY: Penguin Group, 2006.

Thompson, C.W. and Floyd, R.T., *Manual of Structural Kinesiology, Fourteenth Edition.* New York, NY: McGraw Hill, 2001.

Watkins, Matthew, *Useful Mathematical and Physical Formulae.* New York, NY: Walker Publishing Company Inc., 2000.

Body Worlds 2 Exhibit, July 2006 – January 2007 Museum of Science, Boston, Massachusetts.

Printed in the United States
148673LV00004B